dumb things
things
we do

dumb things

things

we do

... in relationships
(and how to make them better!)

Holly Wagner

HarperCollinsPublishers

HarperCollins*Publishers*

First published in the USA in 1999 by WinePress Publishing, Mukilteo, Washington
First published in Australia in 2000
by HarperCollins*Publishers* Pty Limited
ACN 009 913 517
A member of HarperCollins*Publishers* (Australia) Pty Limited Group
http://www.harpercollins.com.au

HarperCollins*Publishers*

25 Ryde Road, Pymble, Sydney, NSW 2073, Australia
31 View Road, Glenfield, Auckland 10, New Zealand
77–85 Fulham Palace Road, London W6 8JB, United Kingdom
Hazelton Lanes, 55 Avenue Road, Suite 2900, Toronto, Ontario M5R 3L2
and 1995 Markham Road, Scarborough, Ontario M1B 5M8, Canada
10 East 53rd Street, New York NY 10022, USA

National Library Cataloguing-in-Publication data:

Wagner, Holly.
    Dumb things we do: in relationships and how to make them better.
    ISBN 0 7322 6694 7.
    1. Married people. 2. Man-woman relationships.
    3. Marriage. I. Title.
306.81

Printed in Australia by Australian Print Group on 79gsm Bulky Paperback

7 6 5 4 3 2 1
03 02 01 00

contents

dumb things she does

dumb things we do

author's note

My husband, Philip, and I have been married for fifteen years — most of them happy ones! In these years we have made plenty of mistakes ... you'll read some of them! Together we pastor The Oasis, a great church in Los Angeles, California. Because pastoring has been our job since we were married, a lot of what I have learned (the good and the bad) about marriage has come as we have worked at the church.

introduction

I was raised watching *Cinderella*, which in itself isn't bad, but I actually believed in the Prince Charming, happily-ever-after stuff. Imagine my surprise when Philip, my husband, didn't always act like Prince Charming. 'Happily-ever-after' came only after serious work and communication and the laying down of my ego. No, that was definitely not mentioned in the fairy tale!

One of my favourite movies is *Sleepless in Seattle*, and after seeing it, one of my girlfriends remarked that a Part Two would be great. I quickly commented that I wasn't too sure it would be an appealing movie because Part Two would just be the couple working out their relationship like the rest of us.

Marriages are crumbling at an alarming rate all over the country and the world. The breakdown of marriages is affecting millions of people in many ways. Not only does divorce affect us emotionally, but it is the number one cause of financial ruin. And so, it is imperative that we do what we can to preserve our marriages and make them strong unions. What I have noticed is that rarely does a marriage fall apart because some outside force has attacked. Even in the case when one spouse leaves the other for another man or woman, that is usually the result of damage that has been done in the marriage months or years earlier. Just as it takes years for a marriage to grow strong and solid, it also takes time for a marriage to fall apart. It is our job as spouses to protect our marriage and to make as many good choices as possible! We hear the minister say at weddings that a man is joined to his wife and the two are to become one flesh. What does this mean anyway?! While we should, in a perfect world, each be whole and healthy emotionally when we begin the adventure of marriage, in reality, we are each like a box of parts. Your husband is a box of pieces and perhaps damaged parts that represent his past up 'til now and you are a box of different, possibly broken pieces and parts. The job you both have now is to each take your box of parts and build something beautiful together. During the building process, making your different parts fit together is not an easy process and it can be quite messy!

So many times in counselling sessions, one spouse will complain that he or she just doesn't love the other spouse any more. I would like to suggest that love is not just a feeling, it is not just a place we fall into, it is not just something we're in — it is something we *do*, regardless of how we feel. Feelings come and go. We can't base our marriages on feelings.

So, let's get ready to look at some of the dumb things we've all done, and see what we can do to bring change. Let's strengthen our relationships so that not only are our homes happier places to be, but also we truly will be a light in a dark world.

dumb things

she does

she does

Chapter One

Not Liking Yourself —

What's Not To Like?

It is not your husband's job to give you a life. It is not his job to make you feel good about yourself. While he wants to be your hero, it is not his job to fix you. We have all heard that we are supposed to 'love our neighbour as we love ourselves'. This means that I won't be effective at loving anyone else if I don't love myself — if I don't love who I was created to be. Philip is not responsible for my self-esteem. I am.

When you like who you are, it makes you more fun to be around. You laugh at mistakes, not taking yourself and

3

everything around you so seriously. You're comfortable with yourself. One evening a few years ago, Philip was speaking at a seminar in our city. I was there with him to be supportive and to talk to the audience about his books and tapes that they could buy to further their education. I was addressing the audience and explaining what was on some of his tapes. It was my first time doing this, and after describing a few tapes, I decided to give some away. I then thought that rather than handing the tape to someone, I would throw it to her. Obviously I need to work on my throwing arm, because instead of the tape reaching the woman I had intended it for, the tape beaned some poor, unsuspecting man in the head.

I felt terrible! My first time on the job, and I blew it! The poor man, with his eyes watering, was trying to be brave as I handed him a tissue, cracked a few jokes on myself, and carried on. (I think my husband slid under his chair at this point!) Now, did I make a mistake? Yes. Have I since learned some cassette-tape distribution etiquette? Yes. Did it rob me of my confidence? No. When you make mistakes and muck up, be willing to laugh. I'm not talking about serious, life-threatening mistakes. Those aren't funny. But sometimes our inability to laugh at ourselves is a sure sign that we lack confidence or self-esteem. We need to learn to like who we are — warts and all!

There are a lot of reasons for low self-esteem. Past abuse, neglect, rejection and abandonment are just a few confidence-stealers. All of us at one point or another have experienced some of these; some of us have experienced devastating abuse. Regardless, the important thing is to begin a plan to build self-esteem. The self-esteem I am talking about is not the self-centred, as-long-as-I'm-happy-it's-OK mentality, nor is it arrogance. I'm talking about the quiet confidence you get from knowing your identity, from knowing you are on the planet for a purpose. There are certainly men who need to understand this, but in my limited experience, I have seen more women struggle with the issue of self-esteem.

According to the 1999 edition of *Time Almanac* there are more than five billion of us on the planet who believe in God. I would like to ask you to take that belief one step further and not only believe in God, but believe that God created you and that it was for a purpose. You are not an accident (no matter what your parents told you!). You were put on the planet at this time in history for a specific reason. You have a destiny, a purpose to fulfil. We won't know our purpose, our destiny, if we don't know our creator.

If I want to know the purpose of my car, or how it was made, I don't ask another car. I ask the company that made the car. When I read the manual I'll know how it works and what all of the buttons are for (not that I'll still be able to do more than put petrol in, but at least I'll know more!).

I would like to suggest that the first step toward liking yourself is to know you were created for a purpose, and that it is a good one. Then I would encourage you to discover what that purpose is by getting to know your creator. You and I were put on this Earth for amazing reasons. We have so much to contribute — so much to share, no matter what our age. We are amazing women and it is not about doing; it is about being.

One of the reasons we must know who we are, is to determine what we'll do. We can't do this backwards. I can't rely on what I do to determine who I am, because if what I do is snatched away or if I fail at it, then I'll see myself as a loser. Evander Holyfield is a phenomenal boxer, but what happens when he can no longer box? He will struggle if his only identity is in being a boxer. What about the Michael Jordans, Julia Robertses and beauty queens of the world? What happens when they can no longer do what they now do? Will they lose personal confidence? Will they be confused or depressed? What about you? Is your identity wrapped up in what you do?

We don't get our identity from our driver's licence; most of the stuff on that is embellished anyway! We don't get our identity from our passport; that just tells us where we've been. We don't get our identity from school reports; most of us are still dealing with the negative things some teachers said. We don't get our identity from a mirror; we just use that to put on make-up. You and I get our identity from our creator. It's through our creator's eyes that we get a true picture of who we are.

We are:

- not victims, but conquerors — in fact, more than conquerors;
- not a loser, but a winner;
- not an addict, but an overcomer;
- not a captive, but set free;
- not a sinner, but forgiven;
- not a random creation, or our parent's 'accident', but put on the Earth 'for such a time as this'.

You can't get self-esteem from reading books, although they're often helpful. You can't get it from going to seminars, although you'll learn a lot. I believe that self-esteem comes, first of all, from living in the identity your creator has given you, regardless of the circumstances. Second, according to Dr Laura Schlessinger in her book *Ten Stupid Things Women Do To Mess Up Their Lives*:

> Self-esteem is earned! When you dare to dream, dare to follow that dream, dare to suffer through the pain, sacrifice, self doubts and friction from the world — when you show such courage and tenacity — you will genuinely impress yourself. Self-esteem is always forged from your efforts.*

One of my weaknesses was not finishing projects once I started them. I am a great starter! It's just my finishing that needs work! Because I saw myself as weak in this area, it affected my self-confidence. I knew I needed a plan. I knew I needed to start something and then actually finish it. At this time in my life, I was taking my son, Jordan, to karate class. As I watched the classes, I began to think, 'I can do this'. Plus, I noticed that at every level a student passed, a new colour of belt was given, all the way to the black belt. It was like a prize, and I like prizes!

So, I signed up for karate. Perhaps this wasn't the easiest of goals for me to reach, but this is what I did. I started as a white belt, and at every class I attended, I looked at the black belt on the wall and said, 'You're mine!' Four years later, I passed my black-belt test. Was it hard? Yes! Were there times I wanted to quit? Yes! Were there times it was inconvenient? Yes! Just the fact that this was a difficult goal to finish made it even more valuable to me. Getting my black belt did things for my self-esteem that nothing else had done up to that point. I had started something and finished it! You can too. Pick something, anything. Find a goal, and begin the process of reaching it. When you do, you will feel amazing!

When a woman is confident in her purpose and has a healthy self-esteem, there is no occasion for envy. Think about it. Why would you be envious of someone else? Because you want what they have, and aren't enjoying who you are. I am always amazed at people who can really sing. I mean, there are women who can actually stay on key for an entire song! It baffles my mind! Because I can't sing a note (or at least not the right note), I could be envious and look at a woman who can sing, wanting what she has. But I would be wasting my valuable time, wanting a talent or ability someone else has instead of being thankful for the abilities I have. None of us was created with the exact same purpose, same personality or same destiny. We are each unique. We each need to spend time discovering who we are and what our purpose is, instead of trying to be like someone else and wanting their gifts. That only leads to frustration and envy. Come on, girls, let's rejoice when one of us accomplishes something, is honoured for a talent she has, or gets married. Don't be envious and wonder why it didn't happen to you. I believe you have been specially created to fulfil a unique purpose. Find out what it is.

A certain proverb asks the question 'Who can find a virtuous woman?' Virtuous, in this context, doesn't mean 'quiet, weak, or able to crochet', which is what I always thought (which is also why being virtuous seemed boring to me!). In my study, however, I discovered that a virtuous woman involves three different qualities bound together. First, the virtuous woman has strength. She is a person with might and valour. She is not a weakling! Second, virtuous actually means 'to be a member of an army'. So, she is a force on the Earth. Look around you; you are part of an

hers

army of women who are walking the journey with you. Third, the virtuous woman has riches, substance, wealth, and knows what to do with it. This woman — you — is amazing.

I am not to wait for a man, my husband, to make me virtuous. No, that responsibility is in my lap. Marriage should be a place where two wholes meet, not a place to get neediness met.

> Make a plan to build your
> confidence in who you are.
> You can do it!

---

* Dr Laura Schlessinger, *Ten Stupid Things Women Do To Mess Up Their Lives*, Harper Perennial, Division of HarperCollins, 10 E. 53rd St. NY, NY 10022.

Chapter Two

NOT DEMONSTRATING RESPECT TO HIM —

R-E-S-P-E-C-T, JUST LIKE THE SONG SAYS!

According to Mr Webster, respect means to show consideration or esteem for. We all should be respected. Respecting one another is part of giving each other the sense of dignity that we all deserve. As you demonstrate respect to those around you, you will find more and more people will open their hearts and lives to you. So, respect is crucial in building healthy relationships. However, I have found, in

hers

talking with many couples, that respect is one of the first things to go. Generally the wife loses respect for her husband or neglects to demonstrate it, and your husband's number one need is to feel respected. He becomes the man he was created to be as he feels he is respected. Of course, there are things he needs to do to earn our respect (I'll talk to him in the other section!), but the thing is, we need to demonstrate respect to our husband, whether he 'deserves' it or not. If there are occasions when you are having a hard time respecting what he does, then respect his position as husband in your home. I don't always respect the decisions the president of our country makes, but I always respect the position of presidency. Likewise, our number one need is to feel loved and the husband is to demonstrate love to us at all times, even when we are unlovable. (Yes, it's hard to believe, but sometimes we are hard to love!) We both have a tough job, because I know there are times when I am not very lovable, but that doesn't change what my husband is asked to do. And there are times when it takes a conscious decision of my will to demonstrate respect to my husband when what I want to do is very loudly give him several pieces of my mind! Nevertheless, my job, because I am committed to building a strong marriage, is to demonstrate respect to my husband.

Let me tell you a story I heard ...

> The mayor of a large city and his wife attended a
> banquet at a hotel. In order to avoid the rush of
> people after it was over, they left the back way and
> walked to their office. On the way, they passed a
> building under construction. One of the construction
> workers yelled out a greeting to the wife. She waved
> and continued walking with her husband. The mayor
> asked his wife who that man was. She replied that he
> had been her boyfriend at one time. Feeling rather
> proud, the mayor asked his wife, 'Aren't you glad you
> married me? Because if you had married him, you
> would've been the wife of a construction worker.' The
> mayor's wife replied, 'No, the truth is, if I had
> married him, he would be mayor.'

This story illustrates the point that, behind every successful
man, there is a woman. I also believe that behind almost
every failure of a man, there is a woman. When a man feels
respected, he can accomplish so much. As women, we have
such an ability to be a great influence in our husband's life.
What an awesome position that is!

If we want our husband to be all he can be, we need to
be an encouragement. When you talk about your husband,

hers

make sure you are speaking in an edifying way. It is very hard for me to be around a woman who is constantly whining and complaining about her husband. My husband has weaknesses. I'm not blind to them or denying them, but I'm not calling my girlfriends and griping, either. I am doing my best to speak uplifting words about him, because I want him to rise to his potential, and I know I have a part to play in that. How are you talking about your husband to your friends and co-workers? We demonstrate respect not only by how we talk about him, but also in how we talk to him.

A certain proverb says 'she opens her mouth with wisdom and on her tongue is the law of kindness.' Kindness literally means 'loyalty'. The words we use should show loyalty to our husband. When you're loyal to someone, you demonstrate that you're on the same team. A sure-fire way for me to start a fight with Philip is for me to come into a conversation, attacking with both guns blazing! (I always carry at least one!) What this proverb is asking us to do is to approach our husband as if we are on the same team. Philip is not my enemy (no matter how many times it has felt like it). He and I should be on the same team, fighting a common enemy — not each other. Look at your heart: do you secretly feel that you are on the opposite team from your husband? Begin to change that. Demonstrate respect by working together to overcome a problem. Demonstrate respect by being loyal.

How you talk to him is so important. A woman I know came to me for advice about an explosive situation with her husband. In the middle of some marital difficulties, she told her husband she had decided to spend a few days alone to get herself together. She did not want to answer the phone or to be with anyone, including friends. Not surprisingly, the husband, who felt like she was demanding something (she was), got angry and resentful. I applauded the woman's desire to spend time working on herself. But I smacked her (not really) for how she handled her desire. She did not demonstrate respect to her husband, but instead demanded something from him. Not surprisingly, he pulled away and became resentful.

I suggested that she go back to her husband, apologise for the way she spoke to him, and ask for what she needed in a respectful, honouring way. I encouraged her to say something like this: 'Honey, I am so sorry for the way I was demanding. I know that wasn't respectful. Please forgive me. [This is called 'eating humble pie' and is often necessary.] I am really feeling overwhelmed right now and know that I am not able to give to you all I should. What would you think if I

hers

were to take a couple of days to rest so that I can get my strength back?'

She must have said something like this, because her husband's response totally changed. When she went to him as if they were members of the same team — who both wanted the best for each other — he responded with love and support. He even offered to get her a hotel room and take any phone messages for her while she was away. He offered to support her in any way necessary. When we are respectful, showing loyalty and demonstrating honour, great things happen.

The key here in showing respect is asking about an issue rather than telling what you are going to do or demanding that something be done. One of the turning points for my friend was that she asked her husband, 'What do you think if I take a couple of days?' She asked him for his input. That opened the door to his heart.

Just as many of you have ideas or suggestions for your husband that you believe would help him at his job, I do too. And so many times as we are leaving our place of work, the church, I will have an opinion about something I noticed in the church that should have been handled differently. I have learned to handle this most delicately! I used to just blast forth with my opinion, assuming my husband wanted to hear it. When I did this, an invisible wall went up, and he didn't hear a thing I said. I realised I needed to do something different if I wanted my husband to hear and receive what I believe was God-given inspiration. The next time I had an opinion about the way something should go in church, I asked Philip if I could share it with him, instead of demanding that he listen.

Now, in spite of my weaknesses, my husband does know that I am his soul mate and so he does want to hear what I have to say. When I asked, he said yes, and then I shared whatever nugget of truth I needed to. He was grateful, and then we talked about the situation. There have been times, however, when I have asked if he wanted to know what I thought and he said, 'No, not now. We'll talk later.' I was OK with that. We need to give our husband the freedom to say no, and not get resentful about it. Because my husband has seen the results of my comments and that my comments aren't necessarily just an opinion, he now asks for my thoughts and input regularly. This is because I don't force them on him. I respect his position enough to ask. So did a great woman of history, Queen Esther, and because she treated her husband with respect, she saved a nation.

hers

Esther became queen, basically because she won a beauty pageant. But she proved to have far more than her beauty going for her. Soon after she was made queen, she found out that her husband's right-hand man, Haman, had devised a plot to kill all of the Jews. Esther, herself a Jew, realised that she needed to do something. In fact, her cousin Mordecai suggested that she was made queen for this cause. First she asked all the Jews to pray. And then, rather than barging in to see her husband, the king, and demanding that something be done about Haman, she invited him to a feast. At the feast, Esther made sure she looked beautiful and that the food was great. At this first feast, she didn't ask anything of the king except that he come back to another banquet. Timing is everything! At this second feast, the king asked Esther what her petition was. She asked him to spare her life, telling him that Haman was plotting to kill all of the Jews, including herself. The king was outraged and had Haman killed, and then as king he provided a way for the Jews to defend themselves.

Because Esther handled the situation in a respectful, honouring fashion, not only was her life saved, but the lives of thousands of Jews were spared. When we begin to demonstrate respect to our husband, not only will he be changed, not only will our relationship be strengthened, but we also will be an example of how to love to all of those watching.

Perhaps you are feeling frustrated because you feel your husband doesn't deserve respect. Don't despair! Find one good thing he does (there should be at least one — after all, you did marry him) and honour him for that. Change how you speak to him, and I believe you will see the results.

> When you demonstrate
> respect to him, he will
> accomplish great things.

Chapter Three

TRYING TO FIX HIM —

NOT THAT HE DOESN'T NEED A GOOD FIXING!

*****

I could hardly wait to marry Philip for a few reasons (one of which had to do with having been celibate for a long time!). Another reason was that he needed some 'fixing', and I was just the girl to do it. Most of us can hardly wait to marry the guy so that we can start changing him. We don't mean anything wrong by our attempts to change him; the relationship is just so important to us that we want to help it in whatever way possible.

John Gray, in his book *Men Are from Mars; Women Are from Venus*, says,

21

> When we try to improve a man, he feels we are trying
> to fix him. The motto of most men is, 'If it's not
> broken, don't fix it.' So if we are trying to fix him,
> he is receiving the message that he is 'broken'.*

Then he starts acting 'broken', which is not what we want! We don't realise that our loving attempts to help him are really disrespectful. (Remember that feeling respected is his number one need.) We think we are just helping him grow and that he is resisting our attempt to improve him. (Actually, he calls it nagging.) We think he is unwilling to change. The truth is, he is resistant to changing because he believes he is not being respected. When a man feels respected, automatically he begins to grow.

Of course there are changes we want him to make; yes, there are areas he needs to grow in, in order to be the ideal husband. However, we can be a help or a hindrance! I have had women coming to me frustrated because their husband isn't fulfilling his role. Sometimes after listening to them for a while, I am not surprised. Daily they were telling their husband what he needed to do, and how he needed to do it. Men will shut down after hearing too much of this. Believe it or not, a man will change — not by how many times you say something, but by your conduct, by your quiet encouragement. It is hard for me to believe that by actually being quiet I can accomplish more than with my many brilliant words, but that is the truth.

We all want our husband to spend what we consider to be an appropriate amount of time with our children. What I've seen, however, is that while they are with the children, we offer all sorts of 'suggestions' about how they should do things. When my son, Jordan, was young, my husband offered to stay with him while I ran some errands. When I got back, I noticed the nappy was on backwards — the little tape tabs were at the back. I quickly pointed this out to my husband and gave him an unasked-for nappy-changing lesson. As time passed, I began to notice that Philip was not offering to change Jordan's nappy very often. I realised what I had done and began to back off. Because, really, what does it matter if the nappy's on backward or upside-down, as long as it's doing its job? And so what if dad feeds the children junk food the night he's got them? Let him be the dad and spend time with them the way he wants.

I had a friend who complained to me that when her husband did the laundry, he put the towels and the sheets in the same load (as if this was a major crime). I would be excited if my husband knew where the washing machine was! I suggested to her that if she ever wanted him to do laundry again, she shouldn't complain, but rather, encourage and be grateful.

I am not quite sure how my husband managed to drive himself around for the thirty-one years before he met me. Once we were married, I began to 'fix' his driving, telling him what streets to take, the quickest way to get somewhere, and stomping my foot on the invisible brake pedal on my side of the car whenever he got too close to another car. When I began to grow in the area of showing respect to my husband by not trying to fix him, it affected many areas of our life. I knew I had to give up my back-seat driving. (I was actually allowed to sit in the front seat after a while!) I also knew it would be tough.

One day we were coming home from church on a route we had travelled hundreds of times. This time, I was determined to be silent, no matter how hard it was. Sure enough, as we came up to the freeway's off-ramp where we needed to exit, my husband sailed right on past it. I bit my tongue as we drove, and drove, and drove miles past our destination. Finally, Philip snapped out of whatever dazed state he had been in and asked, 'Where in the world are we?'

hers

I calmly said, 'Woodland Hills' (which was the next town from ours). We both laughed, but I learned a valuable lesson. (Philip did too.) Actually, he frequently asks me to help in finding a certain location, but I now do it with an entirely different attitude.

Most men usually leave their wife not for someone prettier or for someone with more money but, rather, for some woman who respects him, some woman who thinks he 'hung the moon'. I remember talking to a woman whose husband had just left her. (This obviously was not the best choice for him to make.) She was complaining that he had left her for 'some bimbo who thinks he's just wonderful'. She proudly told me that she hadn't seen him through rose-coloured glasses; she had stood up to him and had challenged him often. She hadn't seen him as some sort of superhero as his new girlfriend did. I actually felt bad for her because her pride was going to be a lonely companion in the years to come. Men need to feel respected. Your husband is looking to be someone's hero. Why not let him be yours?

> Deep inside every man there is a hero or knight in shining armour. More than anything, he wants to succeed in serving and protecting the woman he

loves. When he feels trusted, he is able to tap into this noble part of himself. He becomes more caring. When he doesn't feel trusted, he loses some of his aliveness and energy, and after a while, he can stop caring.

Imagine a knight in shining armour travelling through the countryside. Suddenly he hears a woman crying out in distress. In an instant he comes alive. Urging his horse to a gallop, he races to her castle, where she is trapped by a dragon. The noble knight pulls out his sword and slays the dragon.

As the gates open, he is welcomed and celebrated by the family of the princess and the townspeople. He is invited to live in the town and is acknowledged as a hero. He and the princess fall in love.

A month later, the noble knight goes off on another trip. On his way back, he hears his beloved princess crying out for help. Another dragon has attacked the castle. When the knight arrives, he pulls out his sword to slay the dragon.

Before he swings, the princess cries out from the tower, 'Don't use your sword, use this noose. It will work better.' She throws him the noose and motions to him instructions about how to use it. He hesitantly follows her instructions. The dragon dies and everyone rejoices.

At the celebration dinner, the knight feels he didn't really do anything. Somehow, because he used her noose and didn't use his sword, he doesn't quite feel worthy of the town's trust and admiration. After the event, he is slightly depressed and forgets to shine his armour.

A month later, he goes on yet another trip. As he leaves with his sword, the princess reminds him to be careful and tells him to take the noose. On his way home, he sees yet another dragon attacking the castle. This time he rushes forward with his sword but hesitates, thinking maybe he should use the noose. In that moment of hesitation, the dragon breathes fire and burns his right arm. In confusion, he looks up and sees his princess waving from the castle window. 'Use the poison,' she yells. 'The noose doesn't work.'

She throws him the poison, which he pours into the dragon's mouth, and the dragon dies. Everyone rejoices and celebrates, but the knight feels ashamed.

A month later, he goes on another trip. As he leaves with his sword, the princess reminds him to be careful and to take the noose and the poison. He is annoyed by her suggestions but takes them just in case.

This time on his journey he hears another woman in distress. As he rushes to her call, his depression is lifted and he feels confident and alive. But as he draws his sword to slay the dragon, he again hesitates. He wonders, should I use my sword, the noose, or the poison? What would the princess say?

For a moment he is confused. But then he remembers how he had felt before he knew the princess, back in the days when he only carried a sword. With a burst of renewed confidence he throws away the noose and poison, and charges the dragon with his trusted sword. He slays the dragon and the townspeople rejoice.

The knight in shining armour never returned to his princess. He stayed in this new village and lived happily ever after. He eventually married, but only after making sure his new partner knew nothing about nooses and poisons.

Remembering that within every man is a knight in shining armour is a powerful metaphor to help you remember a man's primary needs. Although a man may

hers

appreciate caring and assistance, sometimes too much of it will lessen his confidence or turn him off.**

Our job is not to fix or change our husband. We are not their teacher (not that there weren't times I didn't try!). That is his job. We are to be the influence, letting our heart, character, and integrity speak for themselves. Come on, women, we can do this! Find a girlfriend who is also committed to respecting her husband as you are, and encourage each other. Help each other in your pursuit of a wonderful marriage.

> ## There are plenty of things in your life to fix; your husband is not one of them.

---

* John Gray, Ph.D., *Men Are from Mars, Women Are from Venus*, New York: HarperCollins, 1992, p. 20.
** *Ibid.*

Chapter Four

NOT GETTING INVOLVED IN WHAT HE'S DOING —

HE REALLY DOES WANT YOU THERE

***** *****

It is good for each of us to have our own interests. In fact, it is very important. Although my husband is a huge part of my life, he is not the only part. That's too much pressure to put on anyone. I should have my own friends, my own interests, and my own goals that all contribute to making me a fun and interesting person. And at the same time, I can't be so busy with 'my life' that Philip and I become

hers

separate, each doing our own thing. It is important to share some areas of life.

My husband is a pastor, and when I met him, while he hadn't started the church yet, I knew that he wanted to be a pastor. When we made the decision to get married, he assured me that he didn't have any preconceived ideas about what a pastor's wife should do. He said that he just wanted me to be his wife and that my role would eventually become evident. He wasn't expecting me to play the piano or sing (good thing!), which is what I thought was the traditional role for a pastor's wife. So, when we first started in the church, I volunteered in many areas, but was always focused on discovering the place I really felt comfortable in. As I grew, and the purpose for my life became clearer, I began to work alongside my husband. I began teaching more and more, and we truly began to share more of the load. Teaching isn't necessarily the role every pastor's wife should fill, but it was a role suited for me. We now share the work and the vision of the ministry.

If your husband is an auto mechanic, you don't necessarily need to know how to fix a car (thank God!), but you should know something about what he does. If your husband is a computer designer or technician, you don't have to understand everything about computers (I certainly don't!), but you should respect his job enough to be able to carry on a conversation, using some computer language. If your husband is a physician or an attorney and belongs to various associations, attend some meetings and functions with him. Find some way to share his job with him, even though you don't have the same job.

Sharing some of the same interests is also important. Philip really likes basketball. Before I met him, I knew what a basketball looked like and the difference between attack and defence, but that was about it (despite the fact that I began my college career at Duke University, which is a big basketball school). Rather than resenting the fact that my husband is a basketball maniac, I decided to join him. I now go to the games with him. In fact, I actually cheer much louder than he does. I know a lot of the players, what teams are doing well, and a lot of the basketball lingo. I knew I had it really bad when during the basketball play-offs, I had the game on the television and Philip wasn't even home!

What is your husband involved in? What is an interest he has that you can share, at least on some level? Read some of the same books. The kind of books that Philip likes aren't necessarily my favourite, but I do read some of them. We have great discussions, and it demonstrates to him that I am interested in him, what he thinks and what he does. At the same time, over the years, he has shown a lot of interest in my pursuits and desires (like sitting through romantic, girl-type movies with me — not just once, either!). While we each have different interests that make us who we are, it is important to find areas of our life that we can share.

Share the work,
and share the fun.

Chapter Five

BEING A DREAM STEALER —

C'MON, CHEER HIM ON GIRLS!

Most people, including your husband, are surrounded by negativity all day. Some of the negativity comes from outside influences, but some comes from inside, springing up from his own self-doubts. He can be bombarded with comments, such as 'that'll never work!' 'No, you can't do that.' 'I don't have what it takes.' 'I'm not qualified to do this.' You and I need to be his encourager — the one who says, 'You can do it! What a great idea!'

I was a cheerleader in high school (remember I'm an American!). Now, the social ramifications that go with that

hers

position today might not be so great, but the honour of being someone's cheerleader is. We should all be our husband's cheerleader! He needs it, and he won't get it from most other people. A cheerleader is someone who speaks encouragement.

The word encourage means 'to put courage in'. Courage means facing danger in spite of fear. As we encourage, we are saying, 'Keep going; keep doing right; you'll get it!' When my son was ten months old, he decided he was ready to walk. I propped him up against a wall, and my husband was ready with the video camera. My son took one little step and then fell on his rear end. I cheered loudly, clapping and telling him what a great job he did. I stood him back up and he began the process again. He took a few faltering steps before he fell. I hugged him, told him how smart he was, and we started again. Now, did I want him to walk like this forever? No. I was actually hoping that, sooner or later, he could string more than two wobbly steps together. But in the meantime, I encouraged every step he made.

As wives, we need to encourage every step our husband is taking in the right direction. He may not be doing something exactly how you want him to, but encourage him along the way. If he is reading books about, and generally working on, his relationship with you, encourage any good thing you see. Instead of complaining about the kind of flowers he brought, thank him! When he says he's coming home early, and it's not as early as you'd hoped for — don't attack him for it as soon as he walks in the door! Be thankful and enjoy the extra time together.

Watch for being critical and impatient, expecting him to get it right immediately. You and I don't always get it right either, so let's dish out the encouragement that we ourselves need. How many of us have ever made a mistake? All of us. Wouldn't it be great if our spouse was cheering us on as we picked ourselves up and started again?

Applaud his dreams and
his attempts to reach them.

Chapter Six

NOT UNDERSTANDING
YOUR ROLE ...

(TAKE A DEEP BREATH BEFORE
READING THIS ONE!)

*****

Believe it or not, there was a time in history when women were considered to be of less value than oxen. Over time, the pendulum swung until we, as women, were told we had to be like men to succeed. The truth is neither of those extremes. I am definitely of more value than an ox and I don't have to be a man, think like a man (really who could?), act like a man or assume a man's role to fulfil my destiny. So what exactly is the role of the woman, especially in marriage?

Throughout history men have traditionally been in a leadership role in the family and the wife in the helper role, submitted if you will, to the husband's position. What does this mean to me today?

Author P.B. Wilson in a recent appearance on the 'Oprah Winfrey Show' talked about her book, *Liberated Through Submission*. Oprah asked what submission meant and the author responded that submission means what the dictionary says it means. It means to yield … yield to people, precepts, and principles that have been placed in our lives as authorities. She went on to explain that throughout our lives someone is always in authority, whether it be our parents, a teacher, an employer, or the president of our country. She then proceeded to paint a picture of what submission looks like by asking us to imagine that there are two vehicles travelling down a freeway. On the right is a semi-trailer truck and on the left a compact car. The vehicles travel side by side for fifteen minutes or so and then a sign appears indicating that the two lanes must merge into one. Based on the *position* of the truck, it has to yield to the compact car. The

hers

semi is stronger, bigger and more powerful. It could force its way. But if it did there would be a collision. And so the semi truck yields to the compact car and they progressively move down the freeway until the lanes open up and they are side by side once again. I thought this to be an interesting picture. Another way to look at submission is the team concept.

On a sports team, there is just one head coach. Imagine the confusion on the team if more than one person was giving the players direction. The coach certainly isn't more important than the players. He just has a different *position*. His job is to recognise the strengths of the different players and to let them do their stuff. His job of creating a championship team is made easier as the players yield, or submit to his direction. When the coach has earned his players' trust, his star players have no trouble submitting to his leadership.

When I was in my twenties and heard the word submission it would make me cringe. It was like fingernails being run down a blackboard. Aagh!! I was raised, probably like many of you, in a generation that was encouraged to challenge authority, and submit to no one. Helen Reddy sang, 'I am woman, hear me roar ...' and it was an appropriate theme song. The feminists were telling me, a well-educated, well-travelled woman, to focus on a chosen career and not to let a family or husband cloud the way. I was encouraged to believe that a career would meet most of my needs. If I still wanted a family, I could do that later — there was always time. While I am grateful for the benefits brought about by the feminists in the workplace and in society, they did not teach me accurately about how to relate to a man and be a part of a husband-wife team. I didn't learn that my family should be my number one priority in order for it to be a successful one.

As a married woman I was trying to figure out my role in the marriage. I knew it had to be somewhat different from Philip's so that we could each bring strengths to the relationship. There had to be a way to make it work, and I set out to find it. I had seen too many marriages blow apart because both the husband and wife were striving to be in charge — neither yielding to the other. I had also seen marriages dissolve because the husband had some weird concept in his mind that his wife should submit to his control and be dominated. The wife didn't take this for very long.

As I listened to author P.B. Wilson talking about submission, at first I didn't like it. However, I did see how submission was crucial in society, in the workplace and in

hers

government. Some of you are employers, and probably good ones who value their employees. Your employees are not inferior to you; they just have a different position and role. Are they less valuable? No. Could you do your job as well without them? No. Do you want your employees fighting for your position? Probably not. While you want them to offer input and suggestions, ultimately you want them to submit to your leadership as the boss. If you are an employee your job is to support your boss, regardless of whether you are male or female.

I met Shanelle about ten years ago while she was attending the University of Southern California. She is a very intelligent woman and soon graduated with an engineering degree. After she had been working for a few months at her first job, which she had been thrilled to get, she came to me complaining about her boss. She claimed that she knew more than he did. He was too hard to work for and didn't listen to her ideas. He never admitted when he was wrong, which was often, nor did he give her credit for good ideas she had come up with. She didn't think she could take it any more. I agreed with her, that it sounded like a difficult situation, and then asked her if she wanted some help in dealing with it — to which she replied, 'Yes.'

Our conversation basically went something like this:

> 'Shanelle, do you believe this is the job that will use your skills effectively?'
>
> 'Yes.'
>
> 'Are there still things you can learn from this company?'
>
> 'Yes.'
>
> 'What do you think your job as an employee is?'
>
> 'I guess it's to do the work I am asked to do and do it well.'
>
> 'Are you doing that?'
>
> 'Well, my boss makes it so hard!'
>
> 'Who said life was easy?? Your job as his employee is to learn from him, to be a good representative of him, to adapt yourself to his requirements, and to be faithful to do good work ... that is if you want promotion.'

She assured me she did want to advance in the company and that she was willing to make some changes in her attitude. It wasn't an easy task, but she began to yield to her boss and be supportive. In a short span of years, she was promoted to the vice-president level of her company, where she was the highest paid woman executive. At every level along the way people saw how hard she worked, for whomever her boss was, and so they kept promoting her. She even bypassed her initial boss. She was promoted time and again over other men and women who didn't understand this concept. She wasn't a doormat. She expressed her opinions whenever they were asked for. She was promoted over men and women who were trying to fight their way to the top, complaining about their bosses all the way. She learned to respect the position of boss, whether or not she ever respected the person as an individual or not. She continued to find favour within the company and with her clients all over the world. Now I believe, as a direct result of her understanding this concept, she was offered and has accepted a position as an officer in the United Nations, where she will have global influence.

As a citizen of the United States I am submitted to the government of our country and its president. Do I necessarily agree with him and the decisions he makes? No, but I must still submit to the *position* of the presidency. I pay taxes and stop at red lights (well, most of them!) because I am submitted to the laws in my country. The motto for the state of Kentucky is 'United we stand, divided we fall'. This is true for any company, my country and my marriage. In a marriage I believe that as wives we are to yield to the *position* of the husband. Now before you start yelling, let me explain what I mean! (If you still want to yell at the end … go ahead!)

Over time I began to see the value in there being just one head in a marriage (a two-headed anything is a monster!). If my husband is the 'coach' then I am his star player! (I think I'm going to ask for a raise!) Perhaps some of you are shuddering at this picture. Why? Why do we scorn submission? Maybe it's because we can only picture the horror of being controlled or abused. Let me make this clear. *No* human has the right to dominate, control or abuse another. No matter what. We need to make a paradigm shift, because I believe what we have always assumed about submission is not accurate.

- Submission is *not* yielding to abuse. If you are in an abusive relationship, get out and get help.
- Submission is *not* being subservient.
- Submission is *not* being a mousy doormat.
- Submission is *not* keeping your mouth shut at all costs.
- Submission is *not* doing whatever you are asked to do even if you are uncomfortable with it.

- Submission is *not* yielding to foolishness or ignorance.

One of the definitions of submission is to make yourself adaptable. Can you adapt yourself so that the team succeeds? It takes a strong woman to do that. One who isn't afraid she's going to lose her own identity. I believe the majority of us who have had a hard time being adaptable — either at home or at work — is because we are concerned that our strengths won't be recognised, or because we'll lose our individual identity. Another definition is to be cooperative. I would like to suggest that for any relationship to succeed the 'we' has to become more important than the 'me'. Cooperation is the key. It can't be 'my way' or 'your way' but instead 'our way'. My marriage, as a unit, is more important than either my individual needs and wants or Philip's individual desires. In a marriage, submission *only* works because the husband has earned the trust of the wife, not because he is more demanding than she is.

There are times when Philip yields to my strengths. In a room full of strangers, I am more outgoing than he is and so in those situations, I take the lead and we make lots of new friends. Maths comes easy for me, therefore I usually am the one doing anything maths-related. Because Philip is confident in who he is, he is not afraid of or threatened by my strengths, but rather encourages them. I recognise that there are men who are not confident in themselves and so attempt to dominate and control. I will talk to them in the other section. Now, while there is no guarantee on how the man will respond, here's a suggestion on how to handle a typical scenario.

'My husband is an idiot at handling the finances. Am I supposed to submit to his ignorance and let him mess us up financially?'

No. Begin a conversation, without attacking, and say something like this: 'Honey, how about if I handle the finances? We'll talk after a month and see if you like what I've done. Because what I'd like to do is strengthen our situation and you have enough on your plate.'

In the previous chapters I have covered topics such as respecting your husband and talking to him in a way that demonstrates that. I have mentioned that trying to fix your husband is not a good idea. And I have talked about the importance of involving yourself in some areas of his life as well as being his number one cheerleader. If you can do these things you are adapting yourself to him and being cooperative, honouring the relationship more than your own comfort zone. Good for you!! Wouldn't our world be a pleasant place to live in if we were all committed to honouring each other and not being so self-centred. I have seen bumper stickers that say, 'Practise random acts of kindness'. What a great world it would be if we actually all did. Submitting, or being adaptable and cooperative, means being kind, preferring the other, letting them go first, be right, win, get the recognition — whatever. We can do this because we are confident in who we are and so are not afraid to give.

If you still feel like yelling, go ahead. You certainly don't have to agree with me on this. I just found that this concept works in my marriage and I have grown and become stronger because of it. If you are married, ask your husband what he thinks. If you are in a relationship, ask the man you are dating. If nothing else, this will provide interesting fodder for a conversation!

Try being adaptable and flexible. See what happens!

dumb things
we do

we do

Chapter One

NOT FORGIVING —

GO AHEAD, SAY 'I'M SORRY'

He who cannot forgive others breaks the bridge
over which he must pass himself.
– GEORGE HERBERT

I'm sure it's taken you a while, but by now you have probably realised that your spouse isn't perfect. And if you are waiting for that spouse to one day be the perfect husband or the perfect wife, you are in for a very long wait. We are all going to make mistakes — some big, some little — as we live out our marriages. I have learned that marriages are built on forgiveness, not on perfection. We need to be quick to forgive each other.

Forgiveness isn't just a nice thing to do. I believe it is a life-and-death issue. I remember talking with a man who had a life-threatening illness. This very ill man was extremely angry with someone who owed him $300. It didn't appear he was going to get his money back, and he was furious, shaking his fists and going red in the face. When I suggested that he go ahead and forgive the debt and the debtor since it didn't look like he was going to be paid back, he became even more angry. Should the debtor have paid his debts? Absolutely. Did the lender deserve to get his money back? Yes. Was it worth his life? I don't think so. I believe the bitterness inside him was killing him.

I have known people dying of cancer or struggling with ulcers who refuse to forgive someone who owes them something, or someone who has betrayed them. They are literally eaten up on the inside with unforgiveness.

Forgiveness can be difficult for us because it pulls against our concept of justice. We want revenge for offences suffered. (Oh, sometimes we won't admit it, but we do!) We want God to bless them with a lightning bolt! You may ask, 'Why should I let them off the hook?' That's the problem:

you're hooked. Or we'll say, 'You don't understand how much they hurt me!' But don't you see? They are still hurting you. You are still living the betrayal, the offence, whatever the crime. You don't forgive someone for their sake; you do it for your sake, so that you can be free.

Forgiveness is pardoning someone. It is letting go of the resentment. Forgiveness is not necessarily forgetting. Forgetting may be the result of forgiveness, but it is never the means. Forgiveness is a choice, a decision of your will. Don't wait until you feel like forgiving to begin the process; you'll never get there. Feelings take time to heal after the choice to forgive has been made.

There have been times when Philip has hurt my feelings by something he has said or done or hasn't done. He's usually aware my feelings are hurt. He would then say, 'I'm sorry your feelings are hurt,' not 'I'm sorry that I hurt your feelings. I was wrong,' which is, of course, what I want him to say. But I don't want any seed of bitterness growing in me, so I choose to forgive. I have also learned that I need to forgive, whether or not Philip says, 'I'm sorry.' (Men, now would be a good time to practise saying 'I'm sorry' out loud. Go ahead. For some reason it seems to be harder for you guys.) My forgiving Philip is not based on whether or not he apologises. Now, of course, he should, and so should I. In fact, we both have got so good at saying 'I'm sorry', we say it no matter whose fault it is. The movie *Love Story* popularised the statement, 'Love means never having to say you're sorry.' Well, I think love is being the first to say you're sorry.

When we hold on to grudges, letting bitterness grow, we begin to withdraw from each other and withhold affection, which will ultimately destroy the relationship. Marriages are about forgiving — daily. If you find that, right now, you are feeling separate from your spouse, I would wager there is some unresolved offence between the two of you. Approach your spouse humbly and without blaming. Describe how you are feeling rather than pointing your finger at him or her.

The ultimate betrayal in a marriage is adultery. If a spouse commits adultery, the spouse who was betrayed has a few choices. First, they can choose to stay. Even though they are angry, they ultimately choose to forgive the betrayal, perhaps getting counselling and working on reconciling the relationship, and all the while, remaining committed to staying. Second, the betrayed spouse can leave.

Most people I have met who have been betrayed by adultery don't really do either. They decide to stay, but instead of forgiving, they begin to withhold affection and love. They make the spouse who committed adultery feel guilty by constantly using the sin against them. While there hasn't been an actual divorce, there has been an emotional one. The betrayed one is trying to punish the offender. They don't want to leave the marriage because that wouldn't be 'right'. Somehow in their mind, staying seems to be a better approach, even though they are angry, withhold love, and are bitter for years. I don't pretend to know the pain involved in this kind of betrayal. What I do know is that whether the betrayed one stays or goes, he or she still must forgive, and get rid of bitterness so that the marriage has a chance of survival, or so that the next relationship isn't tainted with the scars of this one.

I read an article years ago about a couple who was in marriage counselling. The wife was complaining to the counsellor about her husband's 'little black book'. The counsellor, thinking she knew what was in the black book, understood why the wife would be upset. The wife then went on to say that, in this black book, her husband had written down every mistake she had made since the beginning of their marriage, and she just couldn't take it any more.

When I read this I became furious on the wife's behalf, wanting to go after that self-righteous husband. After I had finished muttering about the husband, I heard a small voice say quietly inside me, *you do that too*. I argued that I did no such thing, that I had not written down my husband's mistakes. And then I heard that voice say again, *No, you don't write them down on paper, but you are keeping a record of them in your heart*. I realised that was true. I had been keeping track of all the times Philip had offended me. I made the decision right then to never again keep a record of my husband's wrongdoings. No more keeping score. I was going to be so ready to forgive that I would begin forgiving even before the offence was finished (at least, that's my goal — to be so full of forgiveness).

As human beings, we each need to feel forgiven. We have all made plenty of mistakes in just about every relationship we've ever had. Walking around under the pressure of guilt is no fun. Here's a story that illustrates the great hunger for forgiveness we all have.

The story is told in Spain of a father and his teenage son who had a relationship that had become strained. So the son ran away from home. His father, however, began a search for his rebellious son. Finally, in Madrid, in a last desperate effort to find him, the father put an ad in the newspaper. The ad read: 'Dear Paco, meet me in front of the newspaper office at noon. All is forgiven. I love you. Your father.'

The next day at noon in front of the newspaper office 800 'Pacos' showed up. They were all seeking forgiveness and love from their fathers.*

Let's be people who freely give the forgiveness we all need. In the marriage relationship, we each have specific roles to fill. Husbands, your job is not an easy one, so wives give him a break. He is not going to get it right all the time. Forgive the failures. Cheer the attempts. And husbands, we too have a difficult job. There will be times when we blow it, when we aren't respectful or yielding. Please be quick to forgive and encourage us to try again. Demonstrate forgiveness and love anyway. We will each make mistakes. Give your spouse the forgiveness that you yourself will need — if not now, then the next time you blow it!

Forgiveness is not an easy task. My suggestion would be to first forgive yourself for your own failures. Relationships are not always easy and because we will each make mistakes, not only do we need our spouse's forgiveness, we need our own. Recognise your weaknesses, work on them and forgive yourself when you don't get it right the first, or second or third … time!

Be a great forgiver. The task is difficult, but not impossible. You can do it!

> Be the first to say I'm sorry;
> don't keep a record of offences.

---

* James Hewitt, *Illustrations Unlimited*, Tyndale House, Wheaton, Illinois, 1988.

Chapter Two

Not Fighting Fair —

Yes, There Are Rules!

*****

'You started it!'
'No, you did!'
'No, you did when you changed your mind.'
'Why do you always blame me?'
'I'm outta here!' Slam!

Sounds like a couple of children fighting, doesn't it? Actually, I've heard words like this between adults. No matter how strong the marriage, conflicts will arise. Learning how to deal with them is crucial. Resolving conflicts can strengthen a marriage greatly.

I had a discussion once with a woman who said she and her husband never argued; conflicts never arose in their marriage. As I spent time with them, I noticed this was basically true. I also noticed a total lack of intimacy and honesty, and a superficial level of communication that would eventually lead to trouble or boredom! Resolving conflicts not only opens lines of communication and relieves tension, it also can solve problems, and air differences — all of which are important in strengthening a marriage.

In an argument, often one or both of you are angry. Anger isn't the problem; it's what happens when you're angry that can be problematic. Do you yell, hit, or call each other names? That's abuse, and that's a problem. Do you let your anger push you towards resolving the conflict, or do you attack with it? It is important to learn to manage your anger in resolving conflicts, or you will have bigger problems on your hands.

Just as in global warfare, the Geneva Convention rules are supposed to be followed, in a marriage, there are rules for handling conflict! In any conflict, make sure to stay focused on the issue being brought up. Don't bring out a list of all the things your spouse has done over the years. Unrelated issues are off-limits. Don't blame, accuse, or use words such as 'never' and 'always'. It's better to make the discussion about your personal feelings than it is to point a finger. Use statements such as, 'When —— happens, I feel ——.' Or 'I need ——.' Or 'What would make me feel better is ——.'

Using phrases that begin with 'You should' or 'You need to' or 'You always' will only escalate the conflict. Try to remain calm and logical. You'll get better results if you can express yourself honestly and directly.

Pick your arguments carefully. Don't fight over every little thing! That becomes exhausting and minimises the issues that are really important to you.

Don't start resolving a conflict late at night when you're both tired and emotions are frazzled. It's better to resolve the issue when you are both at your best physically. Unless anger has escalated to rage and you are incapable of managing yourself, then don't leave the room. Commit to continue until the conflict has been resolved, peace is restored, or you have agreed to work it out at another time. It is childish to walk out, slamming doors. Adults resolve issues by seeking peace.

Because most of us aren't that great at effectively resolving issues without causing hurt, I would suggest praying before beginning a discussion that you think could turn into an argument or take time out to make yourself calm. Make a conscious effort so that the words you use will not be careless or hurtful, and that way you may both find peace.

As a general rule, don't argue in front of your children unless you are willing to make up in front of them. It is important for our children to see how we resolve conflicts, not just how we start them. However, I would set very narrow limits on what my children see or hear. There was a couple I knew whose child watched them fight — not resolve conflicts, but fight. The child heard them yelling and calling each other names. If you haven't learned how to resolve conflicts in a calm way, don't fight in front of anyone, and please get some help from a counsellor. Children are helped when they see a mature person resolve a conflict. They are destroyed when they witness the two people who should be providing security yelling and attacking each other.

Conflict resolution is a skill that takes practise and humility. Be willing to take the time needed; be willing to be wrong; and be willing to pray for peace and wisdom. You can do it!

> In a calm manner, focus on the issue at hand, staying committed to resolving the conflict.

Chapter Three

NOT UNDERSTANDING
OUR DIFFERENCES —

VIVA LA DIFFERENCE!

*****

We are each uniquely created with different strengths, different abilities and different personalities. We each have different strengths and weaknesses that need to be dealt with along this journey called life. We need to get good at knowing, understanding and loving the differences, rather then waste time trying to change each other, or waste time wishing each other was different. Carl Rogers said it like this:

63

> When I walk on the beach to watch the sunset, I do
> not call out, 'A little more orange over to the right
> please,' or, 'Would you mind giving us less purple in
> the back?' No, I enjoy the always different sunsets
> as they are. We do well to do the same with people
> we love. *

The reason it is important to understand the differences in our personalities is so that we can function more effectively as a team. Husband, your wife is not you. She won't think or act like you on most occasions. Wife, your husband is not you. He won't respond the same way you would most of the time.

Organisations all over the country are administering personality profiles to their employees, so that employers can better place people in jobs where they would flourish, and so the employees will function better together. It is also helpful to understand the different personality types so that whether we are married or just part of a relationship, we can begin to understand each other. There are many different types of profiles, although they are all basically similar. Hippocrates, hundreds of years ago, developed a system that is helpful and easy to understand. He said there are basically four major personality types.

Every person probably has one dominant personality type and a secondary one, so the combinations are multiplied. No one is put into a box. There is no right or wrong personality. No personality is better than another and each has strengths and weaknesses. Remember, we are learning this to learn how to more effectively love our spouse, and those in our life.

The first personality type I'll talk about is the sanguine. These people are usually the easiest to recognise when walking into a room, because everything about them is moving: their arms, their hands, and their mouth! These people are excited, energetic, spontaneous, and fun-loving. These are the party-waiting-to-happen people, and they can prevent many dull moments. They are outgoing and love to be with people. They can get any project started with a bang. On the other hand, they are not great at finishing those projects. They can forget obligations and can be undisciplined. They often speak without thinking. (Their motto is Ready. Fire. Aim!) Emotionally they need a lot of attention, affection, and approval.

Another personality type is the melancholic. These people are analytical, and like things done perfectly. (White-out and spell-check were invented for them!) They are schedule-oriented and compassionate. They tend to be talented and creative, often genius-prone. Their clothes are enduring (rather than trendy), precise, and have few (if any) wrinkles. (They don't usually like linen.) They can also be hard to please, negative, and depressed over imperfections. Emotionally they need sensitivity, support, and silence.

Quite often these two marry each other. (We did.) I'm the sanguine, and Philip is the melancholic. It doesn't get much more different than that. The great thing is, where I am weak, he is strong and vice versa. However, initially it drove me nuts! He likes all of his 'ducks in a row', and I wasn't even aware there were ducks! I kept trying to make him wrong, thinking that he should have been more like me!

Our closet was an interesting place to work out our differences. His clothes were arranged very neatly. Shirts with short sleeves in one section, then shirts with long sleeves in another, then dark-coloured trousers, light ones, then jeans, and then suits were in their own section. And of course the ties were placed on one spinning rack, and belts on another. Shoes were neatly arranged on shelves. It was an amazing masterpiece! My style of closet management came closer to the 'if when I kicked my shoe off, it hit the doorframe, I called it put away' style. I'm sure that those of you who are melancholics are cringing at the thought of what I did. My husband did too. Gradually, I realised that his organisational skills were a definite strength. He could actually find his clothes in his closet! Rather than continue to call him picky, I let his strength influence my weakness. Now my closet, while it will never be quite as together as his, is vastly more organised. One time, in order to surprise my husband, I installed racks for my shoes. When he came home he was as excited as a melancholic could get. You'd have thought I'd given him a thousand dollars! He has also learned to value my outgoing nature. We meet more people and have more friends because I am such a people person. He likes being with me because I make things more fun. We have learned to value the differences in each other, helping each other overcome weaknesses.

The third personality type is the choleric. This person walks with purpose and focus, never forgetting why they were going from point A to point B. (The sanguine would have stopped to talk to someone along the way, forgetting entirely about point B.) Cholerics can be great leaders, exude confidence, and excel in emergencies. They can see the whole picture and assume leadership where there is none. They can also be impatient and bossy. They have a hard time relaxing and may have a hard time saying 'I'm sorry'. They also might run over people on the way to reach a goal. Emotionally they need loyalty, appreciation, and a sense of control.

The fourth personality type is the phlegmatic. These are the least obvious to identify. They are not extremely anything. They tend to be chameleon-like, capable of adapting in many circumstances. Their clothing is the most relaxed that is acceptable. They are easygoing, sympathetic, good listeners, and make great friends. They are the peacemakers. They can also be unenthusiastic, indecisive, lazy, and resistant to change. (It might take a stick of dynamite to move them to something new.) Emotionally they need peace and quiet, and a lack of stress.

If these two marry each other, they will also have challenges. One wants to be on the go, conquering new goals, and the other wants to quietly do it how they've always done it. The choleric has to be careful not to run over the phlegmatic, but rather learn to appreciate the quiet strength that's offered. And the phlegmatic can learn to try something new and to go to new places.

Whether you have married someone who is very similar to you with a lot of the same strengths and weaknesses (scary thought) or someone quite different, it takes work to go from hating any differences to understanding them, to valuing them. Learn to treasure how your spouse was created.

Don't expect your spouse to be like you. I don't expect Philip to be Mr Social. I know that after he has been at a function for few hours, he's ready for some quiet time. I don't resent this about him, I just accept it. And at the same time, he doesn't resent my need for affection; he has learned to be good at giving it.

Don't hold on to weaknesses saying, 'Well, that's just how I'm made!'. We need to be recognising weaknesses and overcoming them all along the way. We need each other to get the job done.

Discover your unique personality and that of your spouse, and begin working together to form a stronger union.

> ## Treasure the differences in each other, and let them bring strength to the relationship.

---

* Carl Rogers, *Illustrations Unlimited*, James Hewitt, ed., Wheaton, IL: Tyndale House, 1988, p. 338.

Chapter Four

Expect a Great Marriage To Just Happen —

Cinderella Was a Fairy Tale!

I loved Philip. He loved me. Then we both said, 'I do.' I thought that was all it took to have a great marriage: love and a wedding ring. Boy, was I in for a shock after the first month! We all expect our physicians to have gone through years of school and residency in order to be good at what they do, and yet most of us expect to have a strong marriage without ever learning how. Wouldn't it be great if all universities required the students to take a Marriage 101 class? In the long run, that class would certainly prove more useful than the calculus class I took. But for those of us who missed the Marriage 101 class, there is hope!

One of the most important things to do in a marriage is to continue learning how to be a better spouse. It is vital that we continue to grow in our role as a husband or wife, because it is one we will have for a lifetime.

When looking through a microscope, scientists can tell a living organism from an inanimate one by observing any change. If, after a matter of time, there is no growth or change, the object is considered a dead one. It is the same with you and me as individuals and as part of a marriage.

It is important that we grow, both as individuals and as a part of a couple. As individuals, it's important that we be willing to learn new things and think new thoughts. We won't make it through life the way we are supposed to by thinking old thoughts. We need to meet new people, read new books, take new challenges, and set new goals. In other words, we need to be a lifelong student.

I read an article in *Parade* magazine a few years ago that told the story of a group of nuns who consistently lived to be over 100 years of age. Scientists went to their convent to study them and see what was different about how they lived. The scientists got permission to perform autopsies on the nuns who died. During the autopsies, they discovered something interesting. The brains of the nuns had many more connections between different points than most people's brains. These specific connections formed when the brain was learning something new. The scientists then found out, after speaking to some of the nuns, that this group of nuns was continually learning new things, right up until death. They were learning to speak new languages, work new machines, and read new books all the way into their nineties.

Because the brain was continually growing and being used, the nuns lived longer. You and I need to be the type of people who want to learn new things, not just so that our life will be longer, but so that it will be fuller. The growth that I make and the changes I embrace won't change who I am, but they will make me a better me.

As part of a marriage, we need to grow in a couple of ways. We need to be a student of our spouse, not only in learning their personality strengths and weaknesses, but also in learning their likes, dislikes, and needs. We need to learn about them, not to change them but to know them, from the simple, to the more complex — from knowing their favourite food, to knowing what they need when they're hurting. Does he like some space to figure out a problem?

Does she need you to listen to and hold her? Does he like surprises? Does she like everything planned out? What are your husband's dreams, your wife's fears? What is she looking forward to? What is he hoping for? The tricky part about this is you have to be willing and prepared for your spouse to grow and change just as you are doing. Their favourite cereal might change!

As part of a couple, we need to continually be learning about building relationships. I have shelves and shelves of them. I figure that being a wife is one role I will have for the rest of my life, and I want to continually improve at it.

Often people will come to me for some help in their marriage. I am always amazed when I find out that the couple hasn't read a book or listened to a tape on relationships. If they wanted to know how to build a car, they would study and read books on how to do it. Yet most people want to build a great marriage and aren't taking advantage of the wonderful products available. There are conferences, seminars, and retreats available for you to attend. These will provide not only great information, but also a boost that all relationships will enjoy. Please read books, listen to tapes, or go to a seminar. It will definitely be beneficial.

Another way to build a great marriage is to spend time with a couple who has been happily married for longer than you have. I qualified that statement with 'happily', because spending time with people who are down on marriage or negative about their spouse will not be helpful, to say the least. Just as first-time mothers learn from experienced mothers, so we can learn from couples who have been married longer. Find some couples you can spend time with and do it. Extend yourself. You will love the results.

Also, first-time mothers need to spend time with other first-time mothers, so that together they can encourage each other through all the new experiences that come with a baby. Likewise, it's important for us to spend time with couples who are at the same place as we are on the journey of life. There is no replacement for friends who will see you through the obstacles and rejoice with you over the victories. Your marriage will grow and be strengthened as you build relationships with other like-minded couples. Go for it!

> Be committed to growing more as
> a person and as part of a marriage.
> Growth and change produce life.

Chapter Five

ONE LAST THING —

AND I DO MEAN THAT!

Thanks for taking the time to read my book. I hope that the title of this book is not offensive to anyone. I am certainly not saying that any one of you is dumb! However, most of us have done at least one or two dumb things in our life.

My desire is that you will take whatever you learned in these pages and put it to use in your marriage and your relationships. If nothing else, I hope I have given you something to talk about. Also I hope that you will continue to read books on men, women, and marriage. There are many wonderful books out there that can help take your relationship to the next level.

And please take to the time to include God in your marriage. There have been countless studies done and numerous polls taken around the world that prove that making a place for faith in your relationship is amazingly beneficial. Spend time together praying. Perhaps you've seen the billboards that say, 'The family that prays together, stays together'. I would have to agree. When God is on the scene, there is joy, peace, and love. What relationship could survive without those?

I'll leave you with a thought from Howard Whitman:

> It takes guts to stay married ... There will be many crises between the wedding day and the golden anniversary, and the people who make it are heroes. [*]

So, go on, get out there and build the strongest relationship possible.

The dumbest thing we could do is read a book like this and do nothing about it!

---

[*] Howard Whitman, *Philadelphia Sunday Bulletin*, January 15, 1967.

dumb things

things

we do

dedication

This book is dedicated
to those of you reading this;
to those committed to building
a strong marriage in a society
that so desperately needs
to see you succeed.
You can do it!

dumb things

we do

... in relationships
(and how to make them better!)

Holly Wagner

HarperCollinsPublishers

HarperCollins*Publishers*
First published in the USA in 1999 by WinePress Publishing, Mukilteo, Washington
First published in Australia in 2000
by HarperCollins*Publishers* Pty Limited
ACN 009 913 517
A member of HarperCollins*Publishers* (Australia) Pty Limited Group
http://www.harpercollins.com.au

HarperCollins*Publishers*
25 Ryde Road, Pymble, Sydney, NSW 2073, Australia
31 View Road, Glenfield, Auckland 10, New Zealand
77–85 Fulham Palace Road, London W6 8JB, United Kingdom
Hazelton Lanes, 55 Avenue Road, Suite 2900, Toronto, Ontario M5R 3L2
and 1995 Markham Road, Scarborough, Ontario M1B 5M8, Canada
10 East 53rd Street, New York NY 10022, USA

National Library Cataloguing-in-Publication data:

Wagner, Holly.
   Dumb things we do: in relationships and how to make them better.
   ISBN 0 7322 6694 7.
   1. Married people. 2. Man-woman relationships.
   3. Marriage. I. Title.
306.81

Printed in Australia by Australian Print Group on 79gsm Bulky Paperback

7 6 5 4 3 2 1
03 02 01 00

Contents

dumb things he does

preface

'Remind me that divorce is expensive and that murder is against the law!' was a plea I made to a good friend a few years ago. I laugh about that comment now, but back then I wasn't kidding. Not only did it seem that our marriage just wasn't fun any more, but maintaining it was too much work. Perhaps there have been times when you, too, have felt like that. Perhaps you are feeling like that now! Well, take heart; you are not alone, and there are some answers!

In this book I will present some clear, simple suggestions that certainly helped my marriage and that I believe will help yours. This book is not the ultimate guide to wedded bliss; it does not present all the answers to every problem. This book is just a small piece of the puzzle. There are many books on marriage out there; read some. There are wonderful seminars and conferences available to help us married people; go to one. A great marriage doesn't happen just because you want it, but because you want it enough to learn and grow.

I split this book into three sections, 'Dumb Things She Does', 'Dumb Things We Do', and 'Dumb Things He Does'. Read whatever section applies to your situation, or read them all. And after reading, talk. Talk to your spouse about what you've read. Do you agree with this point or that point? Have you done this particular dumb thing? (Let your spouse answer as to whether you have done one of the dumb things or not!) Remember marriages are worked out over a lifetime, so relax ... Even you — no matter how many dumb things you've done — can strengthen your marriage!

dumb
things
he does

Chapter One

NOT LEADING YOUR FAMILY

(WE'RE PLAYING FOLLOW THE LEADER ... YOU!)

Historically men have been given the leadership role in the family. And I believe that when a man isn't functioning properly in this role, chaos ensues. I live in the city of Los Angeles. In certain areas of my city there are thousands of homes where the mother is raising the children on her own. The dad took off for who knows where. The women in these situations are certainly doing the best they can and some of them, on welfare, are managing to motivate their children, giving them a vision to get out of the ghetto. Kudos to these women! But the truth is, they

shouldn't have to. The man should be in the home fulfilling his role, which I believe is leadership.

There are plenty of men around the world who are in absolute rebellion against this concept, and so they are fleeing their responsibilities. I read an article about a famous actor who was quoted as saying that he was divorcing his wife, and basically destroying his family, because this particular time in his life was going to be 'his time'. He wanted to discover 'who he was'. There are times when we all want to abandon what's right and do something just for ourselves. Only, the result of that self-centred action will be grief. This particular actor, on his journey to fulfil his needs, met another young lady and got her pregnant. Now he has another family to abandon. As a man, if you are married, you need to be discovering who you are and what your strengths are from within the marriage. Strengths and weaknesses are revealed under pressure. Let the day-to-day work of your marriage reveal who you are.

I was raised, like a lot of women from my generation, with an attitude that anything a man can do, I can do better. Submission to a husband went out with the bra-burning ceremonies of the seventies! Well, needless to say, I was in for a bit of a shock after I got married. Because not

only are men and women different, but our roles in a marriage are different. And this goes all the way back to Adam and Eve! Before Adam and Eve were banished from the garden of Eden because they ate the apple they were not supposed to, Adam had plenty of leisure time. His toughest job was naming the animals! God provided his food and gave him all he needed, including a wife. After the apple and its consequences, Adam had to work the ground if he wanted to eat and provide for his family. No more fooling around! Now he was called to work, to provide for and lead a wife, who didn't really want to be led.

Part of the consequences in this story that befell Adam and Eve that women deal with is that our desire is for our husband's position of leadership. As women, we are supposed to be adaptable to our husband, even while inside we are battling with wanting the control, with wanting his position. Because of this, I recognise that we are not always easy to lead; however that doesn't change your role.

Likewise, in this story, the consequences for Adam were that he now had to protect and provide for his family when probably he would much rather have been playing. For you, this means that your role is to set the example for your family — not go off and play with the boys, or ?!!? other women.

Leading your family is an active position. Sadly, I have seen so many husbands destroy their families with their own passivity. They aren't watching who or what they let in their home. They are off pursuing some dream, and the wife is the only one bringing in the finances and managing the home. And let me tell you, when a man lets go of the leadership role, we will assume it: and it is not always the best for the family. The wife shouldn't have to do her job as well as yours.

I am aware that for decades we have confused you men until you didn't know what we, as women, really wanted. We hassled you until you became 'soft and sensitive', which is what we thought we wanted. That desire of ours has been changing. I asked some women what quality in a man was the most attractive to them. Most of them answered with words like: confidence, passion, inner strength, ability to make decisions. Those qualities won hands down over: quiet, sensitive, artistic. Not that the latter aren't good traits to have, we just prefer them in smaller doses compared to the first ones mentioned. I apologise now for the confusion we caused.

In our home, as Philip and I were learning about equally important but different roles, things started to go a lot

smoother. If you want your wife to be adaptable and flexible to you, you have to actually lead. Leading *isn't* controlling, being domineering, demanding or bossing anyone around. You must lead by example. If you want your family to be supportive and cooperative, you must be the example. You must give more, love more, be more forgiving and more patient. It's not easy, but you can do it! If you are the coach of the family team, then it is up to you to encourage the strengths you see in your wife ... not be intimidated by them. You are to encourage her strengths and look for ways for her to shine.

Gandhi, a great leader whose actions impacted on the world, didn't lead by demanding or by being controlling — but by serving. He led by example. He brought about global change because he first lived it. Lead your home by setting the example — by serving, not demanding.

Recently Philip and I started taking ballroom-dancing lessons. He took the initiative and signed us up for lessons. At the first lesson, I learned one of the most important rules. Our teacher told us that Philip's job was to lead, and mine was to follow. Imagine that! And even though Philip and I heard her give us the rule, it still took work to act it out. At some point in my growing-up years, I had learned some

dance steps, so I picked up very quickly the dances our teacher was demonstrating. Philip had never done any dancing, so he had a harder time. The temptation for me then was to lead because I knew what we were supposed to do, but our teacher soon stopped that! And she told Philip that in his leading of me, his movements and cues have to be definite not hesitant. If he hesitates, I won't know the right move to make, and we'll end up in a puddle on the floor!

Likewise, husbands, I believe you need to be the leaders of the home — the ones setting the example. If you don't like the results you see in your family, quit blaming and change your actions.

Set a good example in your home.
You can do it!

Chapter Two

NOT KNOWING YOUR JOB —

YOU DO HAVE ONE

O nce you say 'I do' the real work of marriage begins. I know that you may be feeling exhausted from the amazing courtship job you did. You might feel like your job is done. IT IS NOT! Regardless of the work you do outside the home (and us girls are truly grateful for you men who do work and make money!), you do have some very important jobs inside the home.

Love your wife

The number one need of most women is to feel loved. We function at our best when we are well and truly loved, and

we feel that love. It is your job to demonstrate that love (and it is more than sex — although that is definitely a part of it!). Loving your wife means you are as concerned about her future as your own. Loving your wife means you *do* things that show it. Ask her what you can do that will help her feel loved. I can give you some ideas, but you are not married to me — so ask *her*. Actually, just asking her what you can do is a way to show love. It shows you care enough to do something. Sometimes Philip lets me sleep in (I love that!) and he gets the kids ready for school and takes them. It may be a little thing, but I feel loved. He will talk to me for hours about my plans, hopes and dreams — not his, *mine*.

Another little thing — but I feel loved. He will say very nice things about me, in front of me, to other people. A little thing — but I feel loved. And the truth is, he reaps the benefits of me feeling loved. When I feel loved, our sexual relationship is great! When I feel loved, I just want to give and give to him. Loving means doing — look for ways to demonstrate the love you feel. Don't keep it hidden in your heart! Actually, if there are times when you aren't feeling a whole lot of love in your heart, just the actions of doing loving things will bring the feelings back.

Know your wife ... and work toward understanding her!

Plenty of men joke, saying, 'Women — who can understand them?!' Well, you don't have to understand *women* — just one woman, the one you are building an amazing relationship with. It takes work — like all good endeavours that are worth anything — but you can do it!

Work on knowing your wife. What are her dreams, hopes, and fears? What excites her? What hurts her? What makes her cry? Know her.

Another way to know her is to understand that, as a woman, she thinks quite differently from you. We were designed to be different from you, because then, together, we complete the picture. Take the time to study the uniqueness of your wife. The more you understand her as a woman and as an individual, the less likely you are to be angry with her.

Remember, we are not you. We will do most things quite differently, and that doesn't make us wrong.

When we are feeling stressed or hurt by a situation, usually we want your compassion, your understanding. We don't necessarily need you to fix it, so put the tool belt down! One time, my feelings were really hurt by a friend's betrayal. I was devastated. As I sat next to Philip on the couch, he

11

began to give me reasons why I shouldn't feel that way because this person hadn't been a good friend anyway. He said that she had been unsupportive and unfair to me, saying cruel things about me, and so wasn't it good we weren't friends any more? Now, while all of this is true, did this help me deal with my hurt heart? No! What I needed was for him to hold me and let me talk about it. I needed him to say, 'I'm sorry you're hurting. What happened was terrible.' I needed an ear — someone to talk to — not a list of what I should feel and why. Nowadays when I'm hurt or stressed, Philip just holds me and listens and listens and listens! What a guy!

Women are different in so many ways. We talk a lot more than men do. (You've probably noticed this!) By the time you are home from work and winding down, we are just getting warmed up and have a lot more words to say! While your wife should be your friend, she is not your 'buddy'. She needs to be communicated to differently from the way you would to your male pals. One of the reasons we talk is to create intimacy. So when you talk to us, if you would, go a little beyond just the mere facts. You might actually have to string together more words than, 'What's the score?' or 'What's for dinner?' We do want to know your feelings. One of the by-products of intimacy is a great sexual relationship,

which I'm sure you're interested in! So please learn how to communicate your feelings. Ask questions of your wife about her day. Then listen, being patient when she's sharing.

These are just a few ways women are different from men. There are plenty of books out there, explaining in much more detail. Go get one and continue learning!

Your wife probably has a different personality make-up than you do. She probably has strengths where you have weaknesses and weaknesses where you have strengths. Is she outgoing or quiet? Is she organised or spontaneous? What are her strengths? What are her weaknesses, and how can you help her? (It's not by preaching at her or getting angry at her weaknesses!) As you learn to live with and understand your wife, you will make the journey from being angry about the differences to understanding them, to tolerating them, to rejoicing in them!

If you ask young couples if there is anything about their spouse they would change, most will respond with a loud YES! However, I have asked couples who have been married forty years or more what changes they would make in their spouse — and they can't think of one. What happened? I believe they learned to love the differences and be truly glad about them.

Understand your job as
a husband, and even though
it's a challenging one, go
ahead — become great at it!

Chapter Three

NOT GROWING UP —

OK, YOU CAN KEEP YOUR NINTENDO

✳✳✳✳✳

You don't have to put away your Nintendo 64, your surfboard, your roller blades, or your skis, so relax! The growing up that I'm talking about involves thoughts, words, and actions that must change as we grow, if we are to live in successful relationships. You can't be the eternal Peter Pan!

As you build your relationships, you must make the journey of growing from a boy to a man, to a father. There is nothing wrong with each stage, as long as you are committed to moving to the next stage.

A boy is a child. He is entirely focused on getting his needs met. This is not bad, this is what children do. My son, Jordan, is eleven. When he began his life as a baby, Philip and I had to meet all his needs. When he was hungry, we fed him. When his nappy was dirty, we changed it. When he hurt, we held him. We, as his parents, were responsible for seeing that his needs were met.

As he grew, he began to be able to meet his own needs. If he wanted something, he could get it. He wasn't concerned with helping other people get their needs met, but he could take care of his own basic needs and wants. This is not a bad stage to be in. There is nothing wrong with being a boy between the ages of four and thirteen. In fact, that is the only time a person should be a child.

Sometime in those early teen years, the boy should begin the transition to manhood. In many civilisations around the world, this transition is celebrated. In America, with the exception of the Jewish Bar Mitzvah, we don't honour this change. I believe we have a generation of males who are old enough to be men, and yet still act like boys — self-centred and self-indulgent, looking to have their own needs met. When those needs aren't met, they pout, throw tantrums, display uncontrollable anger, hit someone, and slam doors.

This behaviour is not acceptable in my child, and it is disgusting to see in a thirty-year-old male, and yet I have seen it. I have seen males who should be men, displaying all of the above-mentioned behaviours. And if that behaviour doesn't accomplish the desired results, then they play all day, abandon responsibility, don't follow through, and aren't able to make a decision. Being a man means realising the world does not revolve around you. Right now, Philip and I are planning the celebration of our son, Jordan's, transition, during which we will no longer see him as a child or treat him as a child. He will be given more responsibilities, and the training for manhood will begin.

Most of you probably did not have a ceremony or celebration that marked your journey into manhood. In fact, perhaps you were never made aware of the importance of 'putting away childish things', as the saying goes. But, it is never too late to grow up! A boy is concerned with taking care of himself; a man not only takes care of himself, but can do it while also taking care of others. A man is an entirely different person from a boy; he's not just a bigger boy. However, a lot of what we see in our cities are 'boys in men's bodies'.

Because Philip and I live in a city where the entertainment industry is prevalent, we come across a number of people

involved in that industry. I worked as an actress for about fifteen years, and I love the creative, energetic, passionate aspect of that industry. It does, however, perpetuate the boyhood syndrome in some males. Some pursue their dreams at the expense of the real-life priorities. Whether you are pursuing your dream in the area of business, the entertainment industry or even ministry, providing for your family must be a priority.

I heard of an actor who was married and had children. At one point in his career, he was making good money, and then he had a few lean years. Rather than him pursuing other work, his wife had to get a job to bring in finances. She began to be the sole breadwinner, supporting the family while he remained frustrated about having no work. Because he was looking for ways to make himself feel better, he began to spend money on extravagances they could not afford. As this continued, the marriage dissolved.

It is important to have a dream, a vision. If you don't, you will be frustrated, as well as frustrating those around you. However, the dream in your heart should never be at anyone else's expense. I have no problem with the idea of this man's wanting to be an actor, but when the work stopped coming in, it was his responsibility to find other

work. As a man, your job is to take care not only of your needs but those of your family as well.

Perhaps there are many of you who did not have a strong man of integrity as a father to set an example for you. Don't let that be your excuse! There are men in your community who can mentor and support you. There is a men's organisation in America called 'Promise Keepers'. This group draws thousands of men together to work on issues of integrity. Perhaps you could find something similar in your community. Your family is depending on you.

The last transition a male can make is from being a man to being a father. A father is someone who gives to others without expecting anything back. A father gives love when none is coming back. A father is more concerned about his wife's needs than about his own. This is the man so secure in who he is that he can give freely. He's not worried about his own needs being met. A father is not just an older man, but a different person.

Your destiny, your purpose, has been decided. You were not created just to take up space on the planet, but created with a purpose. Your birth was not an accident, no matter what anyone has told you. As you discover the reason for which you have been created, a new strength will rise

within you. You will be able to give freely to others. Remember, your purpose will always include helping other people and will never be at the expense of your family.

I recently heard a song by Randy Travis that asked the question, 'When a tough choice needs to be made, will you make it with the spirit of a boy or the wisdom of a man?'

Discover where you are in your journey. Are you still a boy? It's never too late to grow up. So get started. Drop the tendency toward self-centredness. Find a wise man to whom you can be accountable, and get going! Are you a man making the transition to being a father? Don't give up! Be encouraged. You can do this. You were created to do this. Your family and your world are counting on you to do your part. (No pressure there!)

So, grow up.
Make the journey from boyhood
to manhood to fatherhood.

Chapter Four

Stop Courting Your Wife —

We Want Romance Till We Die!

*****

As women, we have got wise to the fact that you men are conquerors. Most of you feel that after you have put in all the time and effort required to capture us (marry us), you can kick back and relax. Often your passion for romance dwindles a bit. The problem with this is that *our* desire for romance and our need to feel cherished doesn't disappear after the honeymoon! The husband who switches from overdrive romance before the wedding to cruise control after marriage is asking for trouble.

It is very important for a woman, your woman, to feel loved. In fact, feeling loved is our number one need. We are not wrong because we need to feel loved. We are not wrong because we like to be romanced. You might resent our need for love and affection, but it doesn't change the reality that we desire to be cherished. I suggest that, rather than resenting this quality in us, you seek to fulfil the need to the best of your ability — because in a marriage, you are the only one who can!

While the number one need of most women is to feel loved, your wife is probably different from me in how she needs to have love demonstrated to her by her husband. I will make a few suggestions for you, but be sure to check with her to see what she needs. Many times after I have read a book on men or marriage, I ask my husband if the information presented applies to him. I don't want to learn how to be a good wife to the men 'out there' — I want to be a good wife to him.

There are some fairly easy ways to court and romance your wife, and there will be some ways that take a little more work. I love it when Philip brings me flowers for no apparent reason or leaves a note for me to find. But more than the flowers or the note, what touches my heart is that,

his

at some point in his busy day, he took time to stop and think of me. Birthdays and anniversaries are obvious times for romance, but it is the out-of-the-way times that are really meaningful. I know that by bringing flowers or by leaving a note, he is saying, 'I love you. You are important to me.' Sometimes in the middle of the day, I'll get a quick phone call from him, to tell me he loves me. A soft touch, a gentle kiss, a squeeze of the hand as we are both busy about our day really make me feel loved. Little actions like these open my heart.

Most of us have learned over the years that men tend to be visual creatures and women tend to be auditory. This means that you are stimulated or moved primarily by what you see, which is why you like us to shop at 'Victoria's Secret' (a lingerie store) and why we are touched by the words you say. Most high-school boys have figured this out, and unfortunately, some have used this to manipulate a young woman into having sex. They say, 'I love you. That's why I want to sleep with you.' And the young girl, moved by what she hears, not by his physique or lack of one, complies. You can bet I will be teaching my daughter not to believe everything she hears, and that her virginity is priceless.

One of the reasons women talk is to create intimacy and a sense of closeness. Because intimacy for us is linked to what you say, it's important that you don't work all day, then come home and watch television, or work on your car, or work on the computer all night. You might find that we would be a tad unresponsive in the bed. If you want the reward of intimacy, you have to plant the seeds. You have to talk to us.

Romance is important to us, and rather than resent it, just accept it. The occasional gestures, such as a flower, phone call, date, gentle touch, or kind word, go a long way toward creating a happy home. (By occasional, I mean daily!) Try something — anything. Be creative. Find out what she likes.

A few years ago, coming home from church after a Wednesday-night service, Philip told me that he would be leaving for work early the following morning. When I woke up on Thursday morning, he was indeed gone. I began preparing breakfast for our children and getting them ready for school when I noticed an envelope on the table, with my name on it. I opened the envelope and read the note, which said:

Dear Holly,
If you love me, use the enclosed plane ticket and meet me at the top of the Empire State Building at 9:00 p.m. tonight.
[Remember, we live in Los Angeles.]
I love you.
Philip

I read this note a few times and could hardly believe it! Philip, knowing my favorite movie is *Sleepless in Seattle* (a movie in which the couple meets on top of the Empire State Building), and knowing how much I love surprises, had certainly planned one for me. As soon as I stopped jumping up and down, I realised there was another envelope on my kitchen counter. I tore open that envelope and read note number two:

Dear Holly,
What are you doing standing there?
[Now how did he know that?]
You have four hours to get ready. I have arranged someone to take you to the airport and someone to take care of the kids for the 4 days we are gone. We will have at least one fancy night so pack a nice dress!

I have already left for New York, so that I will be there to meet you at the top of the Empire State Building.
Love,
Philip

After I read that note, I was laughing and crying at the same time. I felt so loved. He had planned such a wonderful surprise! Of course, I immediately called my good friends and asked to borrow nice dresses. (Women do this!) Seven o'clock in the morning is not too early for good friends! I got my kids off to school with extra hugs to last the weekend. I was taken to the airport and given a note I was supposed to open on the plane. (I actually waited and did this!) This third note was the sweetest yet. In it, he told me how much he loved me and how much he was looking forward to some days alone with me. He told me he had some fun things planned and that we were going to have a great time. He also wrote that a limousine would be picking me up at the airport and taking me to the Empire State Building. On the plane, I proceeded to share my story with anyone around me who would listen, and by the end of the flight, there were more than a few people excited for me!

his

Once I arrived at New York's JFK airport, the driver met me and ushered me to the awaiting limousine. The music from the movie *Sleepless in Seattle* was playing in the limo. Philip had thought of everything! I was taken to the Empire State Building, and there I met the most wonderful husband in the world! We had four great days — in an exciting city. He had planned things I like to do: high tea in a fancy hotel, a show on Broadway, a carriage ride through Central Park, as well as some things he likes: a Yankee game and a visit to the 'David Letterman Show'. All in all, we had a great time and left (together) more in love than ever.

Now, I understand that this example is a pretty elaborate way to romance your wife. You don't have to come up with something so fancy. In reality, it's the little everyday things that build and strengthen a marriage, although I will admit, a big event every few years can only help! What touched me about the whole New York event was that he did simple things that made it special. Because he knew my favourite movie was *Sleepless in Seattle* he planned our weekend accordingly. He could just as easily have said, 'Holly, how about taking a trip to New York?' Then we would have taken an ordinary

trip. What made it special was the surprise. (I love surprises!)

Your wife is the most important woman in your life; let her know it. I have had a few conversations with some men over the years who were having extramarital affairs. They were spending time, energy, and money, trying to conquer the new woman. If each of these men had taken that time and that energy and had spent it courting his wife, he would have the marriage he wanted. Don't look outside of your home for fulfilment.

I have also known women who weren't feeling loved (our number one need) by their husbands, and so when some smooth-talking man appears, these women are seduced. Should the women have said no? Absolutely! But your job is to keep the walls of your marriage secure; don't leave the door open for trouble to get in. Find out what makes your wife feel loved, and then do it! Do what it takes to have a great marriage!

Here's a funny story that illustrates the unfortunate decline in romance … make sure it's not you!!

A husband's reactions to his wife's colds during seven years of marriage:

his

First year: 'Sugar dumpling, I'm really worried about my girl. You've got a bad sniffle and there's no telling these things, with all the strep throat going around. I'm putting you in the hospital this afternoon for a general checkup and a good rest. I know the food's lousy, but I'll be bringing your meals in from Rozzini's. I've already got it all arranged with the floor superintendent.'

Second year: 'Listen, darling, I don't like the sound of that and I've called Doc Miller to rush over here. Now go to bed like a good girl, just for Poppa.'

Third year: 'Maybe you'd better lie down, honey. Nothing like a little rest when you feel lousy. I'll bring you something. Have we got any canned soup?'

Fourth year: 'Now look, dear, be sensible. After you've fed the kids and got the dishes done and the floor finished, you'd better lie down.'

Fifth year: 'Why don't you take a couple of aspirin?'

Sixth year: 'I wish you'd just gargle or something instead of sitting around barking like a seal all evening.'

Seventh year: 'For Pete's sake, stop sneezing! Are you trying to give me pneumonia?'

Spend some of the same loving energy keeping your wife that you spent getting her! You can do it!

> Make a small gesture today
> to romance your wife, and plan
> a bigger one for the future.

Epilogue

Why It's Great To Be a Guy

*****

OK men, you've done a great job in reading this much. If you are feeling a bit overwhelmed right now, let me leave you with a few thoughts (which were anonymously sent over my e-mail).

Why It's Great to Be a Guy

1. Bathroom lines are 80 per cent shorter.
2. When clicking through the channels, you don't have to stop on every shot of someone crying.
3. You can be showered and ready in ten minutes.
4. Your underwear costs $7.50 for a pack of three.
5. None of your co-workers has the power to make you cry.

6   You can quietly enjoy a car ride from the passenger seat.
7   Three pairs of shoes are more than enough.
8   You don't give a toss if someone doesn't notice your new haircut.
9   You can watch a game in silence for hours without your friend thinking, 'He must be mad at me.'
10 If you retain water, it's in a thermos.

If you are feeling brave, please continue reading this book by turning it over and turning to page 49 to begin reading 'Dumb Things We Do'. Thanks for taking the time!